MW01292181

HOLEY, WHOLLY, HOLY

HOLEY, WHOLLY, HOLY

HOLY

A Lenten Journey Of Refinement

KRIS CAMEALY

Kris Camealy

Columbus, OH

Here is a trustworthy saying that deserves full acceptance: Christ Jesus came into the world to save sinners–of whom I am the worst. But for that very reason I was shown mercy so that in me, the worst of sinners, Christ Jesus might display his unlimited patience as an example for those who would believe on him and receive eternal life.

(1 Timothy 1:15-16)

For sinners like me—may we embrace the grace, that is ours in Christ.

CONTENTS

PART II.
HOW TO USE THIS STUDY

FOREWORD

Constant churning kept me up most nights. It was the nagging feeling I get when I have missed something important. Plus, I couldn't figure out why my mind was whirling with all things Lent related.

Growing up, the practice of Lent was not ingrained in me. Sure I knew enough to get by in casual conversation. I had given up things over the years and had often been creative in preparing my heart for the significance of Easter. Even now, as I sit and try, I can't think of an example worth sharing.

Maybe this year, God wanted me to forgo something substantial. More memorable. This I could do. I could bend lower and sacrifice more. Anything for guilt-free sleep. Only it never came.

Why did I have the impression my Savior wanted more from me? What was I missing and what was Lent all about, anyway? My search engine led me on quite a maze. A road that led to confusion, more questions, and no answers whatsoever. Scary words like penance, repentance, self-denial, and fasting filled my screen. The further I dug, the more overwhelmed I became. This was not working for me.

I sat down at the dining room table instead, hoping to set my heart at ease. Armed with a notepad, pen, and Bible, I began to create my own map. With me at the starting point, the cross at the end, and Lent being the territory in-between. My goal was finding the best path for me. While reaching for my Bible, I recalled a verse I had read recently:

"For Christ also suffered once for sins, the righteous for the unrighteous, to bring you to God. He was put to death in the body but made alive in the Spirit" (1 Peter 3:18 NIV).

It was the "Christ suffered...to bring you to God" part I couldn't get over. And I realized then and there I had always done it wrong. Lent, for me, was always about what I would do for Christ. Me, sacrificing my way to the cross when really I should have focused on Him and how my Savior was going to bring me Home.

My path became clear. I disrobed my ideals, expectations, and all control in one prayer as I told Him I wanted to do whatever it took to become less so He could fill more of me. I was not prepared for what followed. God held up a mirror, and I didn't even recognize myself. Seeing my raw, unedited heart brought shame to a whole new level. Amazing, the things I've held close for so long they appeared foreign when I was able to step back and truly see...me.

Then, I saw a reflection. A glimpse of what He sees in me and all we were working towards on this journey.

A part of me wants to spill my entire Lenten experience

here. Share the ugly, the hard, and the glory found in-between. But this book is not for my story. And it's not about Kris's, either. This is about your season of refinement.

If you asked me to summarize my last Lenten experience, I would say that God stripped me down bare so He could clothe me in the way He'd always planned. And now, when I think of what Christ did for me on that cross, I take it personally. His love and grace came alive. Redemption turned intimate.

I'm actually looking forward to this Lenten season. Those words don't scare me anymore because I know now what awaits on the other side. And Holey, Wholly, Holy explains it brilliantly. My mind keeps trying to imagine how my experience last year would have been different if I had been able to read this book before I began. It would have erased my confusion and aided in creating my map, that much is certain. I like to think it would have saved me some pain. I might have accepted grace sooner, and I am praying this holds true for you.

After reading, what surprised me most was how Kris knew my story so well. I had no idea what I was going through, but there is not one portion here He spared me from. I experienced each one. No shortcuts. Oh how I hope you will say the same.

Holey, Wholly, Holy is not a how-to book on doing Lent well. It's simply a companion's guide to help show you landmarks along the Lenten journey. With you at the starting point, armed with a mirror, and your redemptive self clad in righteousness at the end with a whole lot of you and Jesus in-between. Friend, let Christ bring you to God. This book will get you going in the right direction.

~ Nikki Laven

December 2012

INTRODUCTION

Give up the struggle and the fight; relax in the omnipotence of the Lord Jesus; look up into His lovely face and as you behold Him, He will transform you into His likeness. You do the beholding—He does the transforming. There is no short-cut to holiness. ~Alan Redpath

You Can't Hurry the Holy

Something about the incision site just didn't look right. Having been through two prior cesarean sections, I had a pretty good idea of what things ought to look like as they healed and this definitely wasn't right.

I knew a trip back to the doctor was in order. I also knew that I'd probably caused the problem by pushing myself too hard, too soon after surgery. I justified my increased activity levels because I had two other children who needed me, and well, I'm a mom—it's what I do.

Lying there, exposed on the exam table, I waited and wondered what the verdict would be. More stitches? Glue? Staples? What would it take to put me back together right? The doctor gently poked a bit, eyed the incision site carefully, pulled a bottle of silver nitrate from the drawer

1

and then looking up at me over the top of his glasses said, "Take a deep breath and relax, this is gonna hurt."

The Call

In Luke 4:23, Jesus calls himself "physician," and when we allow Him to, He heals us from the sin-sickness that separates us from Himself. This soul-healing, sanctification process requires endurance, patience, faith, and ultimate surrender to the cross of Christ. Christ calls us to meet Him in Gethsemane and pick up our own cross:

Whoever wants to be my disciple must deny themselves and take up their cross daily and follow me. For whoever wants to save their life will lose it, but whoever loses their life for me will save it. What good is it for someone to gain the whole world, and yet lose or forfeit their very self? (Luke 9:23-25).

Jesus calls us to holiness:

But just as he who called you is holy, so be holy in all you do; for it is written: "Be holy, because I am holy" (1 Peter 1:15-16).

Our life's purpose is to give God glory. We do that by reflecting His image to the world through our worship and our service to His kingdom. By His death He justified us, and through the refining fires He sanctifies us for the work of His purposes. But this refining is a process. You can't hurry the holy.

This book is a collection of short articles written along my own journey of refinement. Some of the writings have been adapted from my personal blog, kriscamealy.com while others are entirely new. I pray you would be encouraged to continue through the fires of refinement and that the peace and joy of Christ would fully envelop you as you strive only to be closer to Him. You do not struggle in vain.

> Friends, when life gets really difficult, don't jump to the conclusion that God isn't on the job. Instead, be glad that you are in the very thick of what Christ experienced. This is a spiritual refining process, with glory just around the corner (1 Peter 4:12-13, MSG, emphasis added).

Glory waits, just around the corner.

BEFORE WE BEGIN

In 2013, when *Holey, Wholly, Holy* slipped from the hidden confines of my hard drive into the wide open space of the world, I hadn't the imagination for what would happen next. What God has done in the years since that first trembling step of obedience, continues to astonish and humble me. In the immediate aftermath of its publication, several readers inquired about a workbook or retreat guide to accompany the book, and a year later, I managed to cobble together and release the *Companion Workbook*. This little book launched a retreat in 2014 (*Refine [the retreat]*), where 20 brave women joined me at a quiet lodge tucked in the woods of Ohio, seeking the refining and healing of Jesus just before Easter. We all came away from that weekend changed, forever impacted by the beautiful, indescribable communion we enjoyed with God. As I write this note now, I am preparing to host another *Refine [the retreat]*, this time, for 50 women. The invitation to discover greater intimacy with God through refinement continues to expand–all by His grace. This project is for me, a constant reminder of one of the many ways God uses our obedience for His greater purposes, and I pray that as you read, you are encouraged to lean in to your own surrender.

My heart for everyone who reads this book and willingly engages with the study and scriptures, is that you too would experience the depths of God's mercy and grace that we did, that budding Spring season in the woods.

This Expanded Reader's edition combines both the original book *and* the companion workbook for your convenience. The work exists in it's original form, with edits being made only to eliminate typographical errors.

Holey, Wholly, Holy is intentionally *not* a 40 day devotional. There are no scheduled readings for each day of Lent. Rather, it is my prayer that you will take your time reading through this book, searching the scriptures, taking the to pray and process your thoughts and insights along the way. My hope is that as you make your way through this season, you will ultimately find your place first, at the cross, and last, at the opening of the empty tomb, rejoicing in the resurrection.

My prayer for you, as we begin:
Father God, you are most perfect and Holy. We cannot fathom the depths of your love that sent your own Son through the horror and suffering of the crucifixion, in place of lowly sinners such as us. Lord as we search for our place alongside you this Lenten season, I ask that you would mercifully lead us into your will, that you would draw us ever closer to your heart, through your gentle humbling. Make us willing Father, help us to receive your grace. In Jesus' name I pray, Amen.

PART I

1

WHY LENT?

Remember that "you are dust and to dust you shall return"
(Genesis 3:19 NLT).

How many years have I walked that center aisle at the beginning of the Lenten season? How many times have I stood silent in line, waiting for the smudging of black ash across my forehead in the shape of a cross? Having grown up in the church, even before I could walk, I likely experienced the marking while carried in my mother's arms. Yet for all the times I've repeated the processional to the altar, the weight of the ashes never settled on me like it did last Lent—and I hadn't even attended the Ash Wednesday service. I found my face to the floor, the weight of the cross bearing down in a way I had never experienced. God stripped me down and, in doing so, brought me to the edge of myself. This book is a result of that intense period of refinement.

A Brief History

The origin of Lent goes back to the time of the Apostles, and though the acceptable practices of the Lenten season have shifted over time, the idea behind the 40 days of Lent stands firm. Lent is traditionally observed for 40 days, from Ash Wednesday to Good Friday, excluding Sundays. The significance of the 40 days most commonly reminds us of the 40 days Jesus spent in the wilderness before the beginning of His short ministry on earth. As the church reflects on Jesus' 40 days in the wilderness, we are called to practice our faith in ways that stretch and bend us beyond what is comfortable.

Generally during Lent, the Christian moves from a period of self-reflection, to confession, to repentance, and finally, to rejoicing in the grace of Christ's resurrection (Easter). In this book, I discuss these four subjects, beginning with self-reflection and culminating with the celebration of grace received through the risen Christ.

This is not meant to be a 40-day devotional, per se, but rather an aid in further reflection on the mystery and mercy of Jesus' death on the cross and His ultimate resurrection. My hope is that you find the readings encouraging and stirring as you draw closer to Christ during your own Lenten journey.

A Personal God

One of the most amazing things about God is how truly personal He is to each of us. Your Lenten journey will not look exactly like mine, and the struggles you face as you allow Him to refine you will be both unique to you as an individual and universal to all of us as members of the human race. It helps to remember that we face no temptation that Christ Himself has not faced:

For we do not have a high priest who is unable to sympathize with our weaknesses, but we have one who has been tempted in every way, just as we are–yet was without sin. Let us then approach the throne of grace with confidence, so that we may receive mercy and find grace to help us in our time of need (Hebrews 4:15-16).

We should find it encouraging that not only does He know the weight of our struggles (and much more so) but He is also with us in the fires of refinement, just as He was with Shadrach, Meshach, and Abednego (Daniel 3:25). He walks with us in the flames and brings us through to the other side.

Come and Die

Traditionally, Lent involves a fast of some variety, with the object of the fast chosen by the practicing individual. Last year, I chose to fast from dessert. (I cringe just writing that.) As I look back at the work God did in my heart, I realize that often times we're only willing to give up the small things—soda, dessert, TV, alcohol, shopping and other completely unnecessary indulgences. The scripture that rung me out regarding what I'm willing to offer up was this one: "You do not delight in sacrifice, or I would bring it; you do not take pleasure in burnt offerings. The sacrifices of God are a broken spirit; a broken and contrite heart, O God, you will not despise" (Psalm 51:16-17).

It occurred to me that perhaps what God calls us to give up, really, is ourselves. The paltry offerings we prefer to give up, while they feel challenging, are perhaps less pleasing because we fail to give up the one thing that stands between us and Christ. Ourselves. Only when we have given up our own ambitions and desires, from that death to self, can we be used to produce much for His kingdom.

John 12:24 explains it this way: "I tell you the truth, unless a kernel of wheat falls to the ground and dies, it remains only a single seed. But if it dies, it produces many seeds."

Have you known the hard seasons of refining? If so, you likely recognize the burn of redemption as it begins to singe away the scales of the sinful life. We are called to live as Christ lived—willing to suffer as He suffered and to be stripped of the excesses and pride that prevent us from living a life that more fully glorifies Him. Dietrich Bonhoeffer said it this way, "When Christ calls a man, He bids him come and die"(Bonhoeffer 89)[1].

As the church is traditionally stripped for the Lenten season, so we, too, find ourselves naked before the Lord, shamed by our awareness of our weaknesses, constant stumbling, and self-righteousness. Jesus suffered all varieties of temptation in the wilderness, and as such, His faithfulness to the Father and His God-nature were put to test. Because He knew no sin (2 Corinthians 5:21), He endured a trial that we could never possibly endure apart from Him. On the cross He took on our shame, and His shame becomes our glory as we allow Him to clothe us in Himself.

In different ways, God tests our faithfulness. He refines

us through trial and suffering so that when we emerge, we might better reflect His glory to the world. We live the Lenten season again and again throughout our lives, as God deals with our sins, and we confess and receive His forgiveness. Easter Sunday may occur once a calendar year, but it is experienced countless times in the Christian's life, as we repeatedly rejoice in the gift of our salvation through the death and resurrection of Jesus. By His good and generous mercy, we can endure hundreds of Lents in this life, as we remember these words found in Isaiah 48:10,11:

See I have refined you, though not as silver; I have tested you
in the furnace of affliction. For my own sake, for my own
sake I do this.....I will not yield my glory to another.

This is the hard refinement, the journey from holey (broken in sin) to wholly (surrendered) to holy. The trials you endure, they are undeniably part of your story—but your life is not just about you—your life is about Christ in you—about the work He can do through you, when you yield to His will.

2

SELF -EXAMINATION (HOLEY)

I know, O Lord, that a man's life is not his own; it is not for a
man to direct his steps.
(Jeremiah 10:23)
It is this: that when we genuinely remember the death we
deserve to die, we will be moved to remember the death the Lord
in fact did die—because He took the place of ours.
(Walter Wangerin, Reliving The Passion)

There's No Shortcut to Holiness

In pursuit of Christ, we stumble into a scary town called
Redemption. We all want to get there, but we prefer to come
in the back alley rather than pass through the muddied
streets under the glaring lights of self-reflection. The cross
in the center of town calls our name, and some of us have
scaled the edges of this place for years. We desperately want
to get beyond it, but we're afraid—we know the path to
redemption requires a trip through refinement.

Shame tells us to duck and cover. Sometimes, the ugly twins, arrogance and pride, hold us back. But the cross burns bright in the center of town; we find ourselves transfixed by the grace of it. Before we know it, we're taking one trembling step after another, hobbling nervously through the filthy streets of our darkest moments.

Shielding your eyes is useless. The only way to it is through it. On the road through Redemption we're forced to see the underbelly of our humanness, the struggle we pretend doesn't exist—the weaknesses we're afraid to show anyone. The blessing and challenge of the journey come through the revelations God gives us about ourselves—and our sins.

The road to Redemption is dangerous. All variety of pit-stops exist along the way, tempting us to linger where we shouldn't—depression, self-pity, unforgiveness, fear, anger, and a variety of other hollows beckon us off the main path.

We must remember, He walks with us—we don't pass through alone. Our silent companion holds our hand and leads us right up the middle of this place. If you've skirted the edges of redemption and longed to get closer to Him, if you've hungered and thirsted for more of the Bread of Life, keep walking. Endure the pain of the refining process because when He has tested you, you will come forth as gold (Job 23:10, paraphrased). You are not alone.

Choosing to Go

When we choose to go, to move closer to Jesus as we are called to do (1 Peter 2:21), we will eventually find ourselves stripped—naked before the Lord as we were intended to be.

This process of moving closer, of growing in Christ, brings with it much pain. And while there's pain in the lessening of ourselves, the deeper blessings more than fill the holes we've spent years trying to cover over. God is big enough. His love is rich enough—but there is no shortcut. There is only the steady, trembling descent into the valley. The question He always asks is, will you go all the way with Him? Will you pursue holiness at the high cost of everything?

A.W. Tozer said, "Complacency is a deadly foe of all spiritual growth. Acute desire must be present or there will be no manifestation of Christ to His people. He waits to be wanted"[4]. Desiring God means we live an active faith, one that looks at a holey life and recognizes that grace can fill the holes. When we experience the fires that refine our faith, we can choose to go through them—to grow through them.

3

COMING DOWN

*"We are brought down to the dust; our bodies cling to the ground.
Rise up and help us; redeem us because of your unfailing love".*
(Psalm 44:25-26)

We begin collecting wounds and piling on scars from birth. Ejected from the safety of the womb, we immediately meet with a sinful world ripe with suffering. We grow and endure hardships of varying degrees from the mildly wounding to the most atrocious cruelty. We survive deep cuts and gashes and sometimes, if we can manage, we block the memories, and the pain dulls just enough.

But God has something better in mind. We can do more than simply limp along—His desire is for us to be complete. He longs to restore us, to strengthen us for the call He places on our lives.

In pursuit of life, of our own dreams, of our own magnificent imaginations, we have a knack for running right into the boiling furnace without even seeing it coming—"We sow on bright clear days the seed of our own destruction."[2]

God's desire for closer relationship with us requires us to be purified. Though He accepts us as we are, He has even better for us. He loves us too much to leave us in our mess. He collects our broken shards and creates beauty from mere fragments, but the process does not come without pain. The truth of the Christian life is that we grow most in our faith through adversity. When our faces are pressed against the dirt, that's when our eyes are most open. The weight of the world presses us lower and it's there, in the spaces where we can scarcely breathe, that we find He is closest, holding our hands, lifting our spirits, filling up the holes in our cracked-up hearts.

Restoration is a process. It's not that He doesn't miraculously heal, certainly there's plenty of testimony to this kind of miraculous, instant healing. But for most of us, soul healing comes slowly—painfully. You'll know it when He's calling you toward His refining fire. The smooth surface you've long stretched over, covering the cracks underneath, begins to ripple from the heat. Memories surface, old wounds begin to weep—the cracks widen and hurts spill.

This is not a time to turn and run, though that may be our instinct. This is the time to stand still, to listen to what He's whispering, and to allow Him to strip you of the covers you've been hiding under. Trust me when I say you've not got anything He hasn't seen before. Stand in this fire, let

Him purify you—this is how He loves us. This is the process of sanctification.

4

ALMOST FORGOTTEN

Christ redeemed us from the curse of the law by becoming a curse for us, for it is written: "Cursed is everyone who is hung on a tree".
(Galatians 3:13)

The memory surfaced out of nowhere. I'd read some other writer's words somewhere in the bowels of the Internet, and suddenly these old images began to fill my mind. It annoyed me, this unexpected intrusion of my past, and I fought hard to make the images stop—but they would not. Without having to even pray about it, I knew these memories resurfacing were from God. I can't really explain it, except that I knew it because the Holy Spirit whispered it somewhere in my hollowed-out-heart. I'd been seeking God harder these days, trying to uncover the reasons for some of my default behaviors. I'd been reluctant to ask Him because, honestly, self-examination is difficult at best and horrifyingly painful at worst. It had already been a bitter Lenten season for me and now, as the end was just a couple of weeks away, I just wanted rest.

God would give me rest, but on His terms and His timing. The memories hung around for days, no matter what efforts I made to block them out. All of my attempts to hide this from God only left me restless and on edge. I knew He was calling me to remember these difficult moments because there was something I needed to see that I hadn't seen at the time.

Finally after a few wrestling days, I relented. "What is it I need to see, Lord?" I demanded. The answer came immediately to mind. It suddenly made shocking sense. Sometimes we are forced to remember our pasts in order to recover from the damage that has been done.

For years, I've struggled with feeling the need to perform to feel worthy. As I tried to lean into God during those long 40 days, something hung heavy on me, making it difficult to be near Him. I resisted my time with Him until His pull became too hard to ignore. Daily, I'd busy myself, trying to dismiss the nagging feeling in my gut to go and sit with the Lord. My fear overcame me. What would He ask me to do? What if I didn't want to know? I have learned that once you acquire the truth, you are then responsible for action. I thought if I just stayed busy enough, God would go away and let me rest. What foolishness.

A Past Redeemed

He'd been pressing on me for weeks, and I recognized

that the refining season wasn't through yet. As He called the images to my mind, I connected the dots. Each face I saw belonged to someone who had rejected me for my unwillingness to perform for them. As a teenager, my budding faith and moral code prevented me from participating in activities which many of my peers chose to engage in. I suffered rejection multiple times as a result of my sensibilities. At the time, despite the pain of repeated rejection, I recovered quickly enough and moved on with my life. I didn't realize these experiences were changing the way I'd behave for years to come.

Yet God knew, and as I wrestled with feelings of failure as an adult, He set me free from the damage of the past. In His goodness, He filled the holes with His mercy and poured in truth to overtake the lies I'd grown to believe. This is the gift of surrender, this is newfound freedom in Christ—a past redeemed.

5

ACHE

"... And by his wounds we are healed"
(Isaiah 53:5).
"But the way of Christ is cross bearing. Christ offers us resurrection power, and hence the hope of renewing rather than losing the old. But the renewal always involves crucifixion. Many of us are too comfortable to be willing."
(Vern Poythress)

We fast from these little things, like dessert or caffeine, and we struggle and crave. Lent teaches us about sacrifice and we think it to be so hard, and while it is, because we are human and frail, our small giving-up is nothing compared to the ultimate sacrifice. Harder than the fast, is the turning of eyes inward, the sifting of filth that settles in the heart, in my heart.

When the shutters have been raised and the light pours in, the self-examination can feel a bit like medieval torture, a brutal pulling and stretching of a soul over the racks of truth. Oh, the brambles that have rooted there, and the indescribable ache in a spirit that has been wounded repeatedly by sins.

There's hollow space left behind when you give something up—a hole aching to be filled. Yet, here, in this painful, holey place—this is where the healing begins. The renewal comes through the wringing out of the soul, through the pulling and dragging out of the ugly—it comes through the sacrifice.

... and by his wounds we are healed" (Isaiah 53:5).

6

ADDITIONAL SCRIPTURE READING

Joel 2:12-14
Mark 1:12-15
1 Corinthians 1:25-30
John 12:20-24

7

CONFESSION

*He who conceals his sins does not prosper, but whoever confesses
and renounces them finds mercy.*
(Proverbs 28:13)
*It is never fun to die. To rip through the dear and tender stuff
of which life is made can never be anything but deeply painful.
Yet that is what the cross did to Jesus, and it is what the cross
would do to every man to set him free.*
(A.W. Tozer)

Get On Your Face

My baby girl says her evening prayers on her face and
the first time she laid low to do it, I knew God was
showing me something. Only days into it, Lent pushed me
to the floor, the sheer weight of my struggle held me down
for 40 days—a full immersion. A sputtering, choking
confession, too long overdue. I'd prayed for resurrection but
first there's the dying that must be endured.

31

God speaks, and I reluctantly heed. I live wracked with sin and a willful spirit that cracks back against the call to bend–to submit, to surrender.

Within the first week or two of the season, I'd consumed Brennan Manning's book, All Is Grace. His words tore me wide open and in the saline bath of confessional tears, I finally lived the baptismal immersion my soul had longed for and desperately needed.

God brought me right down, calling my face to the floor in a most uncomfortable position. These prideful knees resist bending. This Pharisee heart beats self-righteousness with each pulse, and I knew somewhere, eventually, the drop off would come.

Humility is a foreign land that speaks a language I haven't known. Love is humble and in living upright I question if I have ever really loved anything more than me.
There are no bones about it, when I heard the firm whispers there in my closet, indeed, He told me to lay prostrate on the floor.

Here it is. The certain, necessary death, with my face pressed into carpet. I know I've lived a double life–one side of my mouth speaks about obedience while the other side rallies for the independent spirit to "Go!" "Be!" "Do!"
I didn't know Lent would kill me. Thank God for the dying. I find myself walking immersed, neck deep, continually splashing my face with the waters of this faith. Drinking it in, gulping it–gasping for it.
It's all grace and Manning said as much and lived the proof of it, a broken man living a cracked-up life, straddling the

Truth and the flesh. Dying to be remade requires confession. Confession of pride and failures dumped out into the light to be washed away into redemption's gutters, disappearing down drainpipes below.

Beyond the confession, beyond the baptism and the receiving of forgiveness, awaits resurrection. This is the gift, the prize of the hard confessions. I live, a new creation, fresh, wet–washed from the smears of a stiff-backed life. Living full in Christ requires bent knees, bowed heads, humble hearts–confession. And in return He resurrects the dead, breathing new life where only a husk existed. He is risen, and, in Him, we rise.

The God I have come to know loves me as much in a state of disgrace as He loves me in a state of grace, for His compassion is never, never, never based on our performance. It knows no shade of alteration or change. Jesus is the fulfillment of the Isaiah prophecy: the bruised reed of your life He will not crush, and the smoldering wick He will not quench, until He's led the truth of your life's story to victory. This night will you let Him come to you on His terms? Will you let Him love you as you are, and not as you should be? 'Cause nobody... is as they should be.[3]

But he gives more grace. Therefore it says, "God opposes the proud, but gives grace to the humble".
(James 4:6)

8

LET IT BLEED

For the wages of sin is death, but the gift of God is eternal life in
Christ Jesus our Lord.
(Romans 6:23)

I'd prefer to be covered; I'm mostly comfortable with hiding. Most of us are. But there comes a moment when the altar awaits, a beckoning to bare it all—to let the ugly spill out like the guts from a freshly slaughtered lamb.

We stand there, in the pool of it, with the freshness and warmth of the wound still dripping, still spilling–to let God into the mess. This is the hard confession. We lay bare our hearts before the Lord, a cutting of sorts, allowing the poison to bleed out—healing will come.

For the wages of sin is death, and sin we have. We live as repeat offenders. Christ crucified—the absolution for our sins. The sacrificial lamb, broken, poured out—chosen specifically for this purpose. This is His gift. His sacrifice.

We cannot fathom this love. This gift is undeserved, yet still, He's offered up, back broken open, skin raw and our sins bearing down, the weight of it all pressing, thorns piercing His head. He offers it even as we turn our backs and hide, as we disguise our weaknesses for the world—even as we pretend not to need this saving.

He bleeds, and we hide our faces. We are not worthy of this shedding. We don't want to know this, we don't want to see this–and yet we are called to die, to relinquish our very self. C.S. Lewis said of the crucifixion: "Christ died for men precisely because men are not worth dying for; to make them worth it." We look for it now as we wander through the Lenten season–our sacrifice, our learning to die to sin to live with him. We spill the ugly to allow Him to heal the wounds—replacing bits of us with pieces of Himself.

We lift hands and praise Him, as what was once hidden is now revealed. We learn to walk truthfully, no longer damming up the floodgates. We rip the cord and hold on as our true identity gushes out of us—our weaknesses, our failings, our stumbles and our wanderings. All of this, that we might learn to live authentically, honestly before Him, before each other.

There is no shame in brokenness. We are all shattered pieces of the body, just trying to heal up and close the holes that sin leaves behind. Replacing the darkness with light. Hope lives. Resurrection awaits.

9

BRAVE

Your attitude should be the same as that of Christ Jesus: Who, being in very nature God, did not consider equality with God something to be grasped, but made himself nothing, taking the very nature of a servant, being made in human likeness. And being found in appearance as a man, he humbled himself and became obedient to death—even death on a cross!
(Philippians 2:5-8)

I thought that brave meant never giving up. Brave, to me, meant fighting to the death. In a moment of divine intervention, a friend texts me this message—one word: *surrender.*

She didn't know how I needed that word. She didn't know the wrestling I'd been doing with God, or how, as her message lit up the screen in my hand, my heart and soul ached with the weight of original sin. Her word pierced straight through and my shoulders sagged as the word burrowed deep. Surrender. I had fought hard that week. Fought both God and the enemy, a tug-of-war match for the books. I limped into the weekend.

Sometimes bravery looks more like surrender. How on earth this can be I don't fully know, but like everything else in God's economy that runs backwards and inside out to the way I think it should, this somehow makes sense.
I'd grit my teeth and dug in my heels and flat out refused and that one word cracked me wide open at five-thirty on a Thursday afternoon. When it comes to walking closer with Christ, my charging ahead, insisting on braving the way on my own terms isn't bravery, it's foolishness. It's willful disobedience.

To walk closer with Christ, we must bravely surrender to His will, to His discipline, to our independent selves who insist that we can handle life on our own, thankyouverymuch. Turns out, surrendering is harder than bravely pushing ahead.

Your attitude should be the same as that of Christ Jesus: Who, being in very nature God, did not consider equality with God something to be grasped, but made himself nothing, taking the very nature of a servant, being made in human likeness. And being found in appearance as a man, he humbled himself and became obedient to death—even death on a cross! (Philippians 2:5-8)

10

COMING CLEAN

For everyone who exalts himself will be humbled, and he who
humbles himself will be exalted.
(Luke 14:11)

The upheaval of a comfortable life slips in sometimes without notice at first. An unexplained attitude of irritation and tightness of lips, of fists. The Holy Spirit begins to whisper and, like children, we stick our fingers in our ears and flap our tongues in an effort to block it out. We know what's coming. The slow burn of sanctification melts away the edges, and as the fire slips in, we begin to crack. A confession swells and resisting will only lead to more pain. We must bend.

His Word tell us this process is how He really loves us. By loving the filth right out of our hearts, He draws us ever closer and when we release, when we lay low, we can finally hear His heartbeat. Because, when we are lying down in the pit, it's His face we see pressed into the dirt beside us. Lent sometimes comes wrapped in filthy paper with tattered ribbons, sin bound so tight—barbed-wire piercing holes into a heart in need of a good bleed. We must wrestle out the ugly that has for years made a home in the dark festering places.

Reading the words over the Seder meal, "yeast leavens or puffs up, as pride and sin inflates our hearts..." Pride prevents the confession. Pride pushes back grace from whitewashing the muddied up walls we crudely erect within our hearts. I read Luke 14:11, and I wail: "For everyone who exalts himself will be humbled, and he who humbles himself will be exalted."

It doesn't matter that Lent lasts just 40 days. The refining process runs life-long. God knows no timetable except that which He sets by His own hand. He will press us until we come clean. He woos us through flame, with passion and persistence. The grace of it is that, through the scalding, we become renewed. The Father grafts new skin to cover old wounds, and in time we gain wisdom and strength. We become healthier, holier, a little bit more like Christ, and less like us. That is our highest calling.

I'll live in the fires of refinement, if that's what it takes.

11

THE CRUSHING PLACE

Forgive us our sins, for we also forgive everyone who sins against us. And lead us not into temptation.
(Luke 11:4).

The first time I remember confessing anything, I sat across the desk from a graying priest who has neither a face nor a name in my memory. As my "First Communion" drew closer, this apparently was part of the preparation—a face-to-face confession of my sins. I can't recall what I confessed, if anything. I don't remember much besides that.

This memory exists for me in the form of yellow-edged snap-shots from the early 1980s. The memories are mostly still, paused moments of a season when I'm certain life for my parents with three young children was anything but still. But I do recall the awkwardness of this forced confession.

41

I remember the way I shifted uneasily in a giant chair that further dwarfed my seven-year-old self, my toes in black patent leather dangling, swaying nervously above the floor. I remember the shame I felt.

It's been years since that day, and I've racked up thousands of sins since that Sunday. I've deliberately turned my back on God in willful seasons of civil disobedience to His word, to His calling. I've pressed my palms hard flat against my ears and stood with my nose to the wind in blind oblivion to the whirl of the Spirit whipping through my life. I'm good at tightening my lips and clenching my jaw locked-tight.

Confession smelts and causes us to change. True confession comes without coercion. Honest confession before God comes only when the scales have slipped from our hearts and we know, we really see the dark places where we've gone awry. Like our cheap fasts, I'm certain God's not all that interested in our compelled confessions when we are not truly moved in our hearts to lay low before Him. After all, the Lord does not look at the things man looks at. "Man looks at the outward appearance, but the Lord looks at the heart" (1 Samuel 16:7).

Christ had no confession of sins to make. He knew no shame except ours because He bled innocent blood in place of the likes of me. But confession isn't purely for the remission of sins. Confession, as Christ demonstrated in the garden, was a time of emptying before the Lord all that terrifies and troubles us. Confession is a conversation where we remember that He is over all, and our place is under Him.

Before His crucifixion, Jesus spent a night slumped over in desperate prayer, in a garden where this whole story began. Except this garden isn't a paradise on earth. Rather, this garden is named for the pressure of production. This garden is named for the place where fruit dies to become something else. Gethsemane.

I read in Strong's that the word Gethsemane means "the crushing place" or "place where oil is pressed," and the irony (or appropriateness) of such a place setting the scene for Jesus' last night on earth is not lost on me. It's there in this crushing place where Christ shed crimson tears not of water, but of holy blood. His anguish, so intense that as a man He questions the necessity of His impending death, and yet, as the Christ, He simultaneously accepts it out of His perfect obedience to the Father.

As we wander through this Lenten season, we may (and hopefully will) find ourselves at the crushing place. This is a place not for fear, but for freedom. Confession of our doubts and struggles loosens the chains of sin and sends us further into the fires of refinement and deeper on our journey of sanctification. Here in this place, we weep with the anguish of a soul that has seen the depths of our own depravity. We weep with Christ, with honest sorrow and ridiculous joy so that, as we let it all out, we will walk out of the garden freer than when we stumbled in. He takes our filth and nails it to a tree, and the gift is ours when we confess—humbly confess.

12

ADDITIONAL
SCRIPTURE
READINGS

Luke 11:1-9

Mark 14:32-51

Hebrews 12:6-8

1 John 1:9

Proverbs 28:13

Psalm 51:1-5

13

REPENTANCE

This is what the Sovereign Lord, the Holy One of Israel, says: "In repentance and rest is your salvation, in quietness and trust is your strength, but you would have none of it.
(Isaiah 30:15)
But the man who is not afraid to admit everything that he sees to be wrong with himself, and yet recognizes that he may be the object of God's love precisely because of his shortcomings, can begin to be sincere. His sincerity is based on confidence, not in his own illusions about himself, but in the endless, unfailing mercy of God.
(Thomas Merton)

All or Nothing

"And anyone who does not take his cross and follow me is not worthy of me. Whoever finds his life will lose it, and whoever loses his life for my sake will find it" (Matthew 10:38-39).

"When Christ calls a man, He bids him come and die.

It may be a death like that of the first disciples who had to leave home and work to follow Him, or it may be a death like Luther's, who had to leave the monastery and go out into the world. But it is the same death every time—death in Jesus Christ, the death of the old man at his call."

When God kindly asks us to set down our bundle of wants, it's not likely that we refuse Him outright. Rather, we're often good at pretending to submit, while grabbing for the goods when we think He's not looking. With fingers crossed behind our back, we live as if we can operate outside the scope of His vision. The truth is, He doesn't just want our bag of dreams and longings.

His desire is for us to be wholly His, that He might make us holy for Him. With God it's all or nothing. Loving God halfway is the same as not loving Him at all. Loving Him out of mere obligation is equally useless. In Matthew 12:30, Jesus says it this way, "He who is not with me is against me, and he who does not gather with me scatters." These are hard words. We want the blessings without the work. We want the good life without the commitment to maintaining it. We want to win the lottery rather than earn our living.

It's much the same with our faith—with our desire for redemption. We want the gold without the fire—the resurrection without the horror of the cross. But His words are clear. "For [His] sake, we face death all day long" (Psalm 44:22). The only way to get closer to Him is to lie down and die with Him. Daily. When we're stagnant in our faith that usually means it's time to die.

Don't worry, resurrection is coming.

14

FEASTING AND FASTING

It is written: 'Man shall not live on bread alone, but on every
word that comes from the mouth of God.'
(Matthew 4:4)

I've heard many people say they have trouble fasting because of their "issues with food." And I understand this. I do. Food in our culture is far more than sustenance that keeps us upright and moving. Food is entertainment, it's medicine, it's a lover and a friend in the dark of our days when we find ourselves desperately scratching for things to fill the holes. Yes, I'd say we have issues with food.

I find it interesting Satan used food to tempt Eve—food as the mystical elixir that would crown us in glory and knowledge. Poisonous, forbidden food, and yet she ate–sharing her sin with her husband and the rest of us.

Fasting is a practice not to be taken lightly. It is a

spiritual discipline that requires sacrifice, and for some the sacrifice weighs harder than for others. But fasting isn't about food. Fasting is about faith. It is about consciously choosing Christ when we want nothing more than to stuff ourselves with that which is temporary.

Jesus knew temptation. He knew how delicious food looked from His rock in the wilderness, Him with His stomach 40 days empty, rumbling, mouth salivating for something He could sink His teeth into. He knew it and yet He resisted. "After fasting 40 days and 40 nights, he was hungry. The tempter came to him and said, 'If you are the Son of God, tell these stones to become bread.' Jesus answered, 'It is written: 'Man shall not live on bread alone, but on every word that comes from the mouth of God.'" (Matthew 4:2-4).

The Bread of Life

We find fasting difficult because we have grown unaccustomed to the hollow feeling in our bellies. We fill our empty with various things, food or otherwise—anything to mute the pangs that rise up and remind us of our unworthiness, our incompleteness apart from the Father. We gasp, parched and weary and in our soul-starved state, we willingly consume whatever looks good—whatever the tempter dangles in front of our eyes. Still, despite the filling, we live starving.

Apart from Christ, we will make this mistake again and again. On our own we cannot resist. We all stumble and fall short, yet Jesus set the example for us by repeatedly denying the temptations to be more, have more, consume more. We cannot live by bread alone. We need more and this is the very lie we tell ourselves when we say that we cannot fast. But Christ says He is the bread of Life. We say, He's not enough.

We turn and resist the very spiritual practice that will nourish us in a way we cannot fully understand. We deny the words of Philippians 4:13: I can do everything through Him who gives me strength.

God sets the spiritual table and invites the malnourished:

> "Come, all you who are thirsty, come to the waters;
> and you who have no money, come, buy and eat! Come, buy
> wine and milk without money and without cost" (Isaiah 55:1).

He rings His celestial dinner bell and calls us to Himself. He asks nothing, other than that we come- without money, without cost, He implores:

"Listen, listen to me, and eat what is good, and you will delight in the richest of fare" (Isaiah 55:2).

He calls us to come to Him and to eat what is good, what is rich and satisfying. Why not come to Him? Allow yourself to come empty, refraining from that which only gives temporary satisfaction, and let Him fill you.

> "For he satisfies the thirsty and fills the hungry with good
> things" (Psalm 107:9).

*While fasting is a spiritual discipline with much biblical support, some struggle with health concerns that make fasting from food dangerous or perhaps even impossible. Fasts need not be limited to food. Consider your situation,and perhaps consult your physician and determine what you can safely fast from. While we may think of a fast as torturous, the intent is not to cause suffering or illness, but rather that in the absence of the object of our fast, we would draw closer to Christ as we lean into Him for strength. Remember, your heart behind the fast is what matters, not the fasting itself.

For further readings on fasting, see Psalm 69:10, Ezra 8:21-23 Daniel 10:3, Jonah 3:5-10, Isaiah 58:1-14, and Matthew 6:16-18.

15

WHAT DO YOU SEE?

To live by grace means to acknowledge my whole life story, the light side and the dark. In admitting my shadow side I learn who I am and what God's grace means.
(Brennan Manning)

On the Inside

Even though nothing is hidden from God's knowledge, Peter failed to believe the truth of Christ's prediction of his denial. In a way, Peter had already begun to deny the Lordship of Jesus when he refused to believe the words which Jesus spoke to him during the last supper. Of course it's easy to sympathize with Peter. After all, none of us would want to hear from God that we were about to disown Him. Undoubtedly, I have reacted much the same to God's truths that I found difficult to bear.

The truth about who we are apart from Christ can be ugly. Our human nature and tendency towards elevating ourselves above all things make us behave much like Peter did. In looking at Peter's character, we come face to face with ourselves. It's difficult to believe the hard things and so we refuse to hear them, we shut our eyes and our hearts to the truth.

As the Lord refines us, we are called out of hiding. He asks us to come into His light, to bare our truest self. Many of us would rather avoid conversations and situations that expose our vulnerability. But this kind of guarded living doesn't lead to freedom; rather, it tightens the invisible chains with which we are already bound. Simply put, denial stunts our spiritual growth. We have to face the condition of our hearts with open eyes. We have to be willing to see—to accept the truth God reveals about the shape of our souls. There is eternal purpose in mind for this.

As soon as Peter denied Christ the third time, the weight of his sin fell on him. Mark 14: 72 says,

"Then Peter remembered the words Jesus had spoken to him: 'Before the rooster crows twice you will disown me three times.' And he broke down and wept."

The truth of our weakness grieves us. Peter did not want to believe what Jesus had shared with him earlier in the evening, and the reality of this truth broke his heart. We, like Peter, are grieved by our own choices and actions. As Manning says, "none of us are as we should be." The realization of this is a burden we are not intended to carry alone. The truth of this is precisely why we need

Christ—why we need the crucifixion and the resurrection, both His and our own.

Peter's denial of Christ is not the end of the story. The things you find as you inspect the contents of your heart do not reflect the end of your story either. Instead, we can see our shortcomings as a beginning, the place where we open the door and invite Christ all the way in.

He is merciful. He wants to enter in. We don't frighten Him with our messy selves. He longs to bring you through this season stronger, more joy-filled, better able to serve Him and the places and people He has called you to. First things first, open your heart. What has gathered there in the corners?

16

ADMITTING WHERE YOU'VE BEEN

The very first evidence of awakening grace is dissatisfaction with one's self and self-effort and a longing for deliverance from chains of sin that have bound the soul. To own frankly that I am lost and guilty is the prelude to life and peace. It is not a question of a certain depth of grief and sorrow, but simply the recognition and acknowledgment of need that lead one to turn to Christ for refuge. None can perish who put their trust in Him. His grace superabounds above all our sin, and His expiatory work on the cross is so infinitely precious to God that it fully meets all our uncleanness and guilt.[4]

Confession

He stood in front of me, cheeks flushed, his eyes glassy and wide. I knew he'd disobeyed, but he stood there, denying it to my face. I asked him twice, but he held to his lie.

I sent him away, "you need to think about what is happening right now," I told him. A few minutes later, I called him back. "Let's try this again," I suggested. "Tell me what you were doing, and be honest about it." He shrugged, his eyes fixed hard on the floor.

"You already know," he mumbled.

I did know, but I needed him to own it. This was one of those teachable parenting moments that we could not afford to ignore.

"I need you to say it to me, I need you to tell me the truth." I waited silently. His lips trembled as tears leapt from his eyes. With his face still bent towards the floor, the confession spilled out of him. It was as I expected, we both knew it, and still the confession was necessary. Pulling him to my chest I held him in his shame. I forgave him, and in that moment, peace between us was restored.

Jesus' last hours in the garden of Gethsemane serve as a powerful example to us regarding the necessity of honest prayers and communication with God. Though Jesus had no confession to make, He reveals His humanity as He prays fervently in preparation for enduring His crucifixion. His garden prayers are those of deep anguish—rather than an admission of wrongdoing, Christ empties his thoughts and feelings out to His Father.

"My Father, if it is possible, may this cup be taken from me. Yet not as I will, but as you will" (Matthew 26:39).

Jesus tells His disciples that He is "overwhelmed with sorrow to the point of death." Here in the crushing place, He demonstrates what surrender looks like: "Yet not as I will, but as you will."

Though He is clearly troubled by the coming horror of His crucifixion, He demonstrates willing obedience. While most of us will likely never know the terror of facing a literal crucifixion, the death to self (Luke 9:23-24) that God calls each of us to can feel crushing. We have heard someone say that they'd "rather die" than have a certain truth uncovered about them. Maybe we've even said this ourselves. Confession puts us in a state of vulnerability, which for most of us can be so terrifyingly uncomfortable that we avoid it altogether or rationalize away our need to confess at all. After all, Hebrews tells us that God already knows all about our sin: And no creature is hidden from his sight, but all are naked and exposed to the eyes of him to whom we must give account. (Hebrews 4:13).

For some of us, shame tightens the noose around our neck, and we live afraid that our admission of guilt would be the sudden jerk to our death. Confession, however, leads to life. Open, repentant confession before God, serves as the gateway to freedom. Confession allows for forgiveness, which makes us receptive to the redemptive work of Christ. When His mercy infiltrates our hearts we turn from being focused on our sins, to being focused on the Son.

17

TURN

If we claim to be without sin, we deceive ourselves and the truth is not in us. If we confess our sins, he is faithful and just and will forgive us our sins and purify us from all unrighteousness. If we claim we have not sinned, we make him out to be a liar and his word has no place in our lives.
(1 John 1:8-10)

My sense of direction is horrible at best. Add my independent spirit to the mix, and it's no mystery as to how I easily lose my way in certain seasons. At some point, I lost my way. I turned left instead of right, and I stood up too tall when I should have been bent low. I probably made a hundred tiny, seemingly insignificant decisions that nudged me further from the throne. Isn't that how it goes? We live overcome with decisions to make, laziness grabs the wheel, fear slams foot to the floor, and without full awareness we're quickly lost.

Rather than quietly seeking refuge, I stood arrogant and

prideful against the Refiner's fires. Even in writing it, my foolishness insults my own knowledge of what is best. I'm not proud of it, but it's the truth.

While I've hungered for transformation, still I sometimes stand with my heels dug in against the sand, willfully disobedient against getting up, picking up my mat–taking the leap.

How is it possible to forget the character of God? Sin. Deceit. Sour life experiences. These bitter roots cloud the clearest vision when allowed to root and grow in the dark cracks. Despite trying to live life worshiping, the very face of the One I worshiped faded, and slowly my own baggage nearly eclipsed it completely.

> *Lift up your voice with a shout, lift it up, do not be afraid; say*
> *to the towns of Judah,"Here is your God!" (Isaiah 40:9)*

Chasing dreams, following the rules, doing the work—this distracted me from pursuing Him, and then I flat forgot exactly who He is. I've read Isaiah 40 every day this week. Every time I read it, I wept–

> *"He tends his flock like a shepherd: He gathers the lambs in*
> *his arms and carries them close to his heart; he gently leads*
> *those that have young" (Isaiah 40:11).*

The poetry and power used to describe God in this chapter is nothing short of awe-inspiring and deeply humbling. The humbling is what I've needed, the awe is what I'd lost.

"Who has measured the waters in the hollow of his hand, or with the breadth of his hand marked off the heavens?" (Isaiah 40:12)

One day last summer, my littles and I picked a handful of caterpillars off of our broccoli. The kids begged to keep them, so we did. They sat in a jar for a couple of days, and then we watched as their movement slowed and their shape transformed. Three days after collecting them they all slept soundly in their cocoons, transformation in the works.

"He sits enthroned above the circle of the earth, and its people are like grasshoppers. He stretches out the heavens like a canopy, and spreads them out like a tent to live in" (Isaiah 40:22).

Once the caterpillars had no where to go, it seemed there was nothing left to do but let the process begin. At some point, we have to yield to the Father and let Him work in us. We must turn to Him.

"Do you not know?? Have you not heard? The Lord is the everlasting God, the Creator of the ends of the earth. He will not grow tired or weary, and his understanding no one can fathom" (Isaiah 40:28).

Two weeks later, we set 10 butterflies free. I watched hopeful as they lifted off to places they'd never have seen from the ground. Fighting against Him prevents us from experiencing all that He has for us. There's a season for both scrimping along on your belly and fluttering your wings to go higher.

18

METANOEÓ

"But unless you repent, you too will all perish".
(Luke 13:3)

The Greek word Jesus used for *repent* is metanoeó, which when translated means, "to think differently after." This word for repentance is a turning from the old ways of thinking and living, to the new way—Christ's way. This is what we are called to. This changed way of thinking is the mark of true repentance.

Obedient Christian living is marked with repentance. It is not a one-time occurrence. We turn again and again, throughout our lives from the sin that infiltrates our hearts. This turning, this thinking differently afterwards, is the hardline of our faith. We cannot serve two masters, and so in serving Christ we turn from the other idols that vie for our affections. Jesus tells us not to look back. This passage in particular is a straightforward call to utter devotion to Jesus—alone. In pursuing gospel living, we are forced to prioritize our gaze. Christ becomes our home. Our devotion is for Him. He, our sole point of focus.

The fruit of a heart that seeks unity with Christ is a change of perspective. As we wander through the Lenten season, our contemplation of the cross should transform our hearts. The hope is that we would come to think differently than before. The truth is, coming face to face with the reality of a crucified Christ does change our minds. We can no longer look on the cross as a mere symbol of a mythological tale of supposed salvation.

When we imagine our Jesus hanging on that tree, nails split right through His hands and the crown pressed deep into His scalp, bleeding and oozing, when we look on His body there lashed within a fraction of life, skin barely clinging to the bones, muscles exposed and torn from the strain and stretching—we cannot help ourselves but to think differently.

Gazing upon the cross we find our own place in this story. We realize that our view is that of the thief hoisted up there next to Him. We find our identity in the soldiers who mocked Him and in the crowd who demanded His blood and rallied hard for His death. We see that we are not mere spectators in His suffering and death, but in fact are the cause of it.

Walter Wangerin reminds us: "When we genuinely remember the death we deserve to die, we will be moved to remember the death the Lord in fact did die—because His took the place of ours."5 We come away from this scene with a hunger to live as He lived. Paul writes in Ephesians 5:1-2:

"Be imitators of God, therefore, as dearly loved children and live a life of love, just as Christ loved us and gave himself up for us as a fragrant offering and sacrifice to God."

This living as Christ, exemplifies our repentance and reveals a mind and heart transformed—that we would no longer live as those hiding from the fires of refinement, but would instead fling ourselves willingly into His furnace. We can trust Him to bring us forth sanctified, redeemed for His purposes. There is no greater glory than a life lived to honor the Lord. Tozer said, "The man who has God for His treasure has all things in one."

May we never strive for anything other than a life marked by repentance, may we go forward from this Lenten season thinking differently than before.

Metanoeó.

19

ADDITIONAL SCRIPTURE READING

Ezekiel 33:11
Luke 24:47
2 Peter 3:9
Matthew 3:1-8

20

ATONEMENT

His divine power has given us everything we need for life and
godliness through our knowledge of him who called us by his own
glory and goodness. Through these he has given us his very great
and precious promises, so that through them you may participate
in the divine nature and escape the corruption in the world
caused by evil desires.

(2 Peter 1:4)

God the Holy One is the source of life; sinfulness separates us
from the holiness and so separates us from life. Holiness is a return
to Eden's ideal and a taste of paradise. The holy life is a foretaste
of heaven on earth. It is not God's burden for us but God's best for
us.

(Simon Ponsonby)

Anything

The hard refining had begun to ease, the heat grew less intense and as I thumbed through an old journal, I saw the words I'd scrawled out, "Lord remove my pride." I'd forgotten that prayer. I mean, I've muttered and wept and sighed a great many prayers in my life, I can't possibly recount them all, and yet, God never forgets a one of them.

All this time with my face in the carpet I didn't know He was answering a prayer. He's dependable. In His omnipotence He chooses when and how to fulfill the cries of a heart that longs for Him.

I'd prayed the "anything prayer," the one that says "have your way with me Lord, do anything that would bring you glory." Had I not believed He would? Or maybe I believed but imagined the process would be cleaner, less painful, less heartbreaking. His ways are not our ways, and when our life is so rapt with our selfish ambitions, we don't always let go neatly.

What we can't always see in the heat of change in progress is the glory that awaits. I wasn't actively seeking refinement. God chose the time and process according to His purposes and not my own. A great many times in our Christian life we will endure hard times. Those times are always a preparation for the next thing. The unseen.

We are no good to God when we're playing God ourselves. How can we serve and love and reflect Christ when we begin and end with ourselves? The refinement is not to be feared or resisted. We can walk willingly into the fires because He's already been there, He goes there still. What we find in the lower places of repentance is a God who knows us with all of our ugly on the inside and yet He cups our faces in the filth and lifts us. He lifts us up as we set the weight of the baggage we carry down.

The journey through Lent is a journey that doesn't end

at the cross. *No!* This journey ends at the empty tomb when we realize that He's beaten back death. This journey ends in the victory of grace for sinners and redemption for those who believe. We find Jesus walking on the road and comforting those who mourn. We find Him with pierced hands outstretched encouraging us to poke our own fingers into His holy spaces and see that He is real—that He lives and because He lives, *we live.*

In resisting the cross, in running from time in the tomb, we risk missing the greatest glory that ever existed—resurrection. There's no greater hope than knowing that in time, we will be raised with Him—on earth, as it is in heaven. He picks us up from the ashes, as one journey ends a new one begins. Your hard refinement is not the end, but rather a new beginning. He's calling you out for more than this. He's preparing you for glory, friends, for *His* glory.

21

WEAR THE ROBE

*I delight greatly in the Lord; my soul rejoices in my God. For he
has clothed me with garments of salvation and arrayed me in a
robe of righteousness, as a bridegroom adorns his head like a
priest, and as a bride adorns herself with her jewels.*
(Isaiah 6:10)

Wearing holy righteousness feels sometimes like a robe
that doesn't fit. Knowing the depths of my depravity, I
recognize my inferiority. But that's precisely the point. As
the sun rises on the empty tomb, we discover a Christ who
overcomes the hindrance of death to proclaim everlasting
life.

We find through Him this same offer extended to us, and
in fact it's more glorious because while He took on death
which He never deserved, we deserve eternal punishment
and can escape it. In His generous mercy, He offers to cover
our sins with His holy robe.

Grace overtakes a sin-wrecked life and makes us holy. I

wrestled this grace to the ground and I'm thankful to say that because I lost, I won. After a hard season of refining, where God repeatedly revealed my broken places, I couldn't bear the weight of this undeserved covering. My shame was too great, as was my pride.

In humility, we must allow Him to drape it over us. No, we don't deserve it. We can't afford it, for the cost is innocent blood shed for its purchase—and yet it's ours for the taking. What glory! What grace!

We can endure the process of sanctification because we are called to live. God is the source of all life and thus He calls us to Himself. We could not bridge the gap if not for the crucified Christ. Alleluia! He lives, and in Him we live!

The God who made the world and everything in it is the Lord of heaven and earth and does not live in temples built by hands. And he is not served by human hands, as if he needed anything, because he himself gives all men life and breath and everything else. From one man he made every nation of men, that they should inhabit the whole earth; and he determined the times set for them and the exact places where they should live. God did this so that men would seek him and perhaps reach out for him and find him, though he is not far from each one of us. 'For in him we live and move and have our being.' As some of your own poets have said, 'We are his offspring' (Acts 17:24-28).

22

BY HIS STRENGTH, FOR HIS GLORY

Some time ago, I started signing things with this little phrase, "by His strength, for His glory." In my desperate prayers to be more like Him, less like me, I realized (or rather perhaps God revealed to me) that the only way to redemption is by His strength, and it's always for His glory. Not only is this the only path to redemption, but it's also the only way worthy of living the Christian life.

As we grow through our refining, we realize that we live and breathe because of His grace, not our goodness or ability. Our life exists because he breathed it into purpose by His own strength, and for His ultimate glory. As "little Christs," we're called to live as examples of God's love on earth—a light for the world, the salt of the earth.

Living redeemed is impossible without the strength of Christ in us. It's not for our own glory we serve, but rather for His glory, that all might see Him in us and praise Him, rather than us. We're to be a mirror reflecting the true source. 1Peter talks about this in reference to how we ought to use our gifts to serve:

> Each one should use whatever gift he has received to serve others, faithfully administering God's grace in its various forms. If anyone speaks, he should do it as one speaking the very words of God. If anyone serves, he should do it with the strength God provides, so that in all things God may be praised through Jesus Christ. To him be the glory and the power for ever and ever. Amen. (1 Peter 4:10-11)

He refines us that we might shine brighter for Him. And it's by His strength, for His glory—because ultimately it isn't about us. We endure the hard refining for the Father's glory, as it says here in John:

> "He cuts off every branch in me that bears no fruit, while every branch that does bear fruit, he prunes so that it will be even more fruitful. This is to my Father's glory that you bear much fruit showing yourselves to be my disciples." (15:2,8)

I've wrestled continually with this prickly temptation to turn everything around to be about me. This is the reason I blame others for my struggles and shirk difficult responsibilities—this is the reason I battle selfishness and pride. Even when the refining process first noticeably began last year, I tried again and again to make it about me. But it isn't. God doesn't just purify us so we'll be a better wife, or friend, or mother. Those are more side-effects than purpose.

He prunes us so we will bear fruit. For Him. For His kingdom, not ours. Our faith is purified so that God will be glorified.

> *Praise be to the God and Father of our Lord Jesus Christ! In his great mercy he has given us new birth into a living hope through the resurrection of Jesus Christ from the dead, and into an inheritance that can never perish, spoil or fade—kept in heaven for you, who through faith are shielded by God's power until the coming of the salvation that is ready to be revealed in the last time. In this you greatly rejoice, though now for a little while you may have had to suffer grief in all kinds of trials. These have come so that your faith—of greater worth than gold, which perishes even though refined by fire—may be proved genuine and may result in praise, glory and honor when Jesus Christ is revealed (1 Peter 1:3-7).*

Obviously God wants us to be the best people we can be. He wants us to love our families and neighbors as He loves them. But even that isn't about us. Loving like Christ means loving selflessly, even unto death. The only way to get it right is to give the glory to Him. The call to refinement for the Christian is not about making us look better, it's about us reflecting Christ better.

Redemption's a dirty town. The filth of our lives piles up in the gutters and some days, we sell little bits of our soul to avoid walking through it. But there's only one way to the other side, and every alley ends up the same place. For most of us, Redemption's a ghost town, a desert that ought to be crossed in a few days, but some of us will take years to get through. It's not a race. There's no rushing the process along. Obedience is critical, humility necessary, and prayer and communion are the sustenance for the journey.

"Dear friends, do not be surprised at the painful trials you are suffering as though something strange were happening to you, but rejoice that you participate in the sufferings of Christ, so that you may be overjoyed when his glory is revealed" (1 Peter 4:12).

PART II

HOW TO USE
THIS STUDY

The content in this study guide is structured in much the same way as *Holey, Wholly, Holy: A Lenten Journey of Refinement*. Each section corresponds to its labeled section in the book and includes study questions and scriptural support for the ideas expressed. Take your time to answer each question fully and honestly. The refining process is often hindered by our unwillingness to be ruthlessly honest about where we are on our journey. The content of this study can be a bit intense for some. Step into the presence of God knowing that your secrets are not secrets to Him. He knows you on a level that no one else does—let this be a comfort to you as you begin to unpack your stuff.

There is no time limit or constraint on completing this study, and I caution you against setting those types of boundaries during the process. Because the refining process never actually ends until we are united with Christ in glory, it may be helpful to identify a couple of key areas where you distinctly notice God speaking to you, and focus on those as you work through the guide.

Though the scripture passages have been included, this

is primarily for your convenient reference. You will benefit the most from the study by taking the time to read the passages in context in your preferred translation.

23

PREFACE

In His book, The Ragamuffin Gospel, the late Brennan Manning quoted Gerald May, a Christian Psychiatrist, as saying, "Honesty before God requires the most fundamental risk of faith we can take: the risk that God is good, that God does love us unconditionally. It is in taking this risk that we rediscover our dignity. To bring the truth of ourselves, just as we are, to God, just as God is, is the most dignified thing we can do in this life."

The catalyst for change always begins with a willingness to be real about where we currently are.

My life has been forever altered as a result of embracing a new kind of honesty before God. There is an indescribable freedom that comes from admitting that sometimes—most times, I am a bit of a mess. I am allowed to be "in-process" because God is continually refining me and melting away the impurities that keep me from reflecting Him. I continue to pray for God to open our eyes to our sin, to take us down the winding road of redemption so we can emerge healed, and strengthened for His service. Our wholeness can only be found in Christ.

24

SEEK YE FIRST

We wake to the buzzing of emails and calendar reminders rolling in on our smart phones. Before our feet have even hit the floor, 35 percent of us will have spent time on our handheld device, playing catch up before the sun has even risen. Once out of bed, we scurry from appointment to appointment. A hundred different things call to our attention and divert us in every direction. I wonder how God can work with a mind that's so fragmented and distracted.

We spend an average of 10 minutes a day looking for something we've lost or misplaced. That's 3,650 minutes or roughly 60 hours a year spent trying to find something. How much time do we spend looking for Jesus?

Only thirteen percent of "Bible readers" as classified by the Barna Group (people who read the Bible 3 – 4 times per year) claim to read their Bible every day.

Of all the time we spend looking for lost things and scrolling mindlessly through a steady stream of social media and technical wizardry, how much time do we devote to seeking God?

We're busy people. We're a humming culture, a hive of constant activity. But the intention for all of us is that we would seek God first.

Traditionally, Lent is a time of intentional seeking and spiritual reflection. This dim season allows for the purposeful slowing of our pace, to ponder the truest state of our heart and our life.

Where are we going in such a rush and why? What are we misplacing in the blur of activity? How much time will we lose trying to recover these things? It's more than lost keys and misplaced cell phone adapters. When we ignore the pull of God on our lives, we risk losing our very souls. There's not enough time in eternity to find it once it's lost. Whether or not you participate in a fast during the Lenten season, whether or not your participation in Lent is new or habit, we must first seek Him.

In Matthew chapter 6, Jesus gives his disciples many instructions on how to live out their faith. He covers a variety of concerns, like how to pray, how to fast, and how to give. He encourages them to trust and not worry, and He tells them how to bring their requests before God.

Seek first His kingdom and His righteousness and all these things will be given to you as well (Matthew 6:33).

With all the distractions that surround us, Christ tells us that to gain the things we need, we must seek Him first. While this particular passage begins with Jesus pointing to how our physical needs will be met by seeking Him first, I can point to a wealth of scriptures that proclaim how seeking God also serves as the means to meeting our non-physical needs.

Scriptural reasons to seek God:

because you WILL find Him (Deuteronomy 4:29)

because He loves those who seek Him (Proverbs 8:17)

because He hears and restores us (Jeremiah 29:12-14)

because the Lord is good to those who seek Him (Lamentations 3:25)

because when you seek Him, you WILL find Him (Matthew 7:7-8)

because those who seek the Lord lack no good thing (Psalm 34:10)

because He rewards those who seek Him (Hebrews 11:6)

because He will forgive you (2 Chronicles 7:14)

because He will draw near to you (James 4:8)

Of course this is only a short list. Many more references outline the benefits of seeking God— I could have made this section shorter by simply saying, we must seek the Lord because Jesus said so. But if you're anything like me, sometimes even that isn't reason enough to do something. The refining process is not a passive happening. It is shockingly easy to become distracted and disengaged from the heart work God is doing when we decline opportunities to actively, and intentionally, seek Him.

As He lovingly pursues us in this process, so we too must constantly watch and listen for His presence. We must seek Him. First. In each portion of this study we will begin by seeking Him first through prayer. We will ask God to reveal His truth to us because we will not come to know

His plan and His direction on our own. As Proverbs 2:6 reminds us—wisdom comes from the Lord, For the Lord gives wisdom; from His mouth come knowledge and understanding.

Join me in seeking Him.

25

WHAT DO YOU SEE (SELF-EXAMINATION)

To live by grace means to acknowledge my whole life story, the light side and the dark. In admitting my shadow side I learn who I am and what God's grace means.

~Brennan Manning

Pray

Gracious God, open my eyes that I may see as if for the first time. Open my heart to receive both your love and gentle correction. And may I know the fullness of your grace through these revelations. Lord, grant me your wisdom. Amen.

ON THE INSIDE

Even though nothing is hidden from God's knowledge, Peter failed to believe the truth of Christ's prediction of his denial. In a way, Peter had already begun to deny the Lordship of Jesus when he refused to believe the words which Jesus spoke to him during the last supper. Of course it's easy to sympathize with Peter. After all, none of us would want to hear from God that we were about to disown Him. Undoubtedly, I have reacted much the same to God's truths that I found difficult to bear.

The truth about who we are apart from Christ can be ugly. Our human nature and tendency towards elevating ourselves above all things make us behave much like Peter did. In looking at Peter's character, we come face to face with ourselves. It's difficult to believe the hard things and so we refuse to hear them, we shut our eyes and our hearts to the truth. As the Lord refines us, we are called out of hiding. He asks us to come into His light, to bare our truest self. Many of us would rather avoid conversations and situations that expose our vulnerability. But this kind of guarded living doesn't lead to freedom; rather, it tightens the invisible chains with which we are already bound. Simply put, denial stunts our spiritual growth. We have to face the condition of our hearts with open eyes. We have to be willing to see—to accept the truth God reveals about the shape of our souls.

There is eternal purpose in mind for this. As soon as Peter denied Christ the third time, the weight of his sin fell on him. Mark 14: 72 says,

> *"Then Peter remembered the words Jesus had spoken to him: 'Before the rooster crows twice you will disown me three times.' And he broke down and wept."*

The truth of our weakness grieves us. Peter did not want

to believe what Jesus had shared with him earlier in the evening, and the reality of this truth broke his heart. We, like Peter, are grieved by our own choices and actions. As Manning says, "none of us are as we should be." The realization of this is a burden we are not intended to carry alone. The truth of this is precisely why we need Christ—why we need the crucifixion and the resurrection, both His and our own.

Peter's denial of Christ is not the end of the story. The things you find as you inspect the contents of your heart do not reflect the end of your story either. Instead, we can see our shortcomings as a beginning, the place where we open the door and invite Christ all the way in. He is merciful. He wants to enter in. We don't frighten Him with our messy selves. He longs to bring you through this season stronger, more joy-filled, better able to serve Him and the places and people He has called you to. First things first, open your heart. What has gathered there in the corners?

READ & REFLECT

READ MARK 14:27-31 AND 14:66-72

And Jesus said to them, "You will all fall away, for it is written, 'I will strike the shepherd, and the sheep will be scattered.' But after I am raised up, I will go before you to Galilee." Peter said to him, "Even though they all fall away, I will not." And Jesus said to him, "Truly, I tell you, this very night, before the rooster crows twice, you will deny me three times." But he said emphatically, "If I must die with you, I will not deny you." And they all said the same. ... And as Peter was below in the courtyard, one of the servant girls of the high priest came, and seeing Peter warming himself, she looked at him and said, "You also were with the Nazarene, Jesus." But he denied it, saying, "I neither know nor understand what you mean." And he went out into the gateway and the rooster crowed. And the servant girl saw him and began again to say to the bystanders, "This man is one of them." But again he denied it. And after a little while the bystanders again said to Peter, "Certainly you are one of them, for you are a Galilean." But he began to invoke a curse on himself and to swear, "I do not know this man of whom you speak." And immediately the rooster crowed a second time. And Peter remembered how Jesus had said to him, "Before the rooster crows twice, you will deny me three times." And he broke down and wept.

1. Peter was forced to confront the truth about his heart when he turned his back on Christ, just as Jesus had predicted. What image comes to mind when you read this passage? What emotions do you feel? Can you sympathize with Peter?

Think of a time when you realized something about yourself that pained you to acknowledge. How did this realization come about? What did you do with the truth you uncovered? (Confess it, seek healing, etc.)

READ JOEL 2:12-14

"Yet even now," declares the Lord, "return to me with all your heart, with fasting, with weeping, and with mourning;

and rend your hearts and not your garments." Return to the Lord your God, for he is gracious and merciful, slow to anger, and abounding in steadfast love; and he relents over disaster. Who knows whether he will not turn and relent, and leave a blessing behind him, a grain offering and a drink offering for the Lord your God?

2. What is the call to action in the very first verse?

3. How do you feel about the intensity with which this call is issued?

4. What is it that God wants from His people?

5. God tells the Israelites to rend (tear, or cut out, Greek translation) their hearts rather than their garments. God is not impressed with our misplaced grief and our public displays of surrender. We are challenged to live in genuine surrender, true submission to God's will. Have you surrendered your heart to Him, or are you merely "putting on a show" of your faith?

6. Take a few minutes to pray. Ask God to reveal the things you are holding back from Him. Ask Him to open your eyes so that you can return to Him fully. List some of the things He reveals below.

7. What response can we expect from God as we lay our hearts bare before Him?

8. God is not threatened by our wayward ways. In spite of our shortcomings, He woos us back to Himself to receive His mercy and love. Do you believe the truths stated about the character of God in Joel 2:13-14? Have you experienced His mercy and pity for the hearts of His wayward children? Describe what that experience was like.

9. God asks for our hearts. He wants deep fellowship with us. Knowing that this is how we are called to live, we must ask ourselves this one question: will we let God all the way in? Will you?

10. If you find it difficult to say "yes" to this question, take a bit of time to pray about whatever it is that causes you to hesitate. Identify and list the issues that are stumbling blocks to stepping forward in faith (fear, disappointment, anger, anxiety, distrust, etc.).

When we choose to go, to move closer to Jesus as we are called to do (1 Peter 2:21), we will eventually find ourselves stripped—naked before the Lord as we were intended to be. This process of moving closer, of growing in Christ, brings with it much pain. And while there's pain in the lessening of ourselves, the deeper blessings more than fill the holes we've spent years trying to cover over. God is big enough. His love is rich enough—but there is no shortcut. There is only the steady, trembling descent into the valley. The question He always asks is, will you go all the way with Him? Will you pursue holiness at the high cost of everything?

Prayer Prompts

Thank God for His generous patience and mercy. Name specific instances that come to mind where you have experienced this.

Ask God to reveal the places where you doubt His word. Ask Him to open your heart to receive His truth, even as it challenges you.

Pray for the strength to claim Jesus as Lord of your life, whatever the circumstances you may face.

26

ADMITTING WHERE YOU'VE BEEN (CONFESSION)

The very first evidence of awakening grace is dissatisfaction with one's self and self-effort and a longing for deliverance from chains of sin that have bound the soul. To own frankly that I am lost and guilty is the prelude to life and peace. It is not a question of a certain depth of grief and sorrow, but simply the recognition and acknowledgment of need that lead one to turn to Christ for refuge. None can perish who put their trust in Him. His grace superabounds above all our sin, and His expiatory work on the cross is so infinitely precious to God that it fully meets all our uncleanness and guilt.
-Harry Ironside

PRAY

Have mercy on me, O God, according to your unfailing love; according to your great compassion blot out my transgressions. Wash away all my iniquity and cleanse me from my sin. For I know my transgressions, and my sin is always before me. Against you, you only, have I sinned and done what is evil in your sight; so you are right in your verdict and justified when you judge. Surely I was sinful at birth, sinful from the time my mother conceived me. Yet you desired faithfulness even in the womb; you taught me wisdom in that secret place. Cleanse me with hyssop, and I will be clean; wash me, and I will be whiter than snow. Let me hear joy and gladness; let the bones you have crushed rejoice. Hide your face from my sins and blot out all my iniquity. Create in me a pure heart, O God, and renew a steadfast spirit within me. Do not cast me from your presence or take your Holy Spirit from me. Restore to me the joy of your salvation and grant me a willing spirit, to sustain me. Then I will teach transgressors your ways, so that sinners will turn back to you. Deliver me from the guilt of bloodshed, O God, you who are God my Savior, and my tongue will sing of your righteousness. Open my lips, Lord, and my mouth will declare your praise. You do not delight in sacrifice, or I would bring it; you do not take pleasure in burnt offerings. My sacrifice, O God, is a broken spirit; a broken and contrite heart you, God, will not despise. May it please you to prosper Zion, to build up the walls of Jerusalem. Then you will delight in the sacrifices of the righteous, in burnt offerings offered whole; then bulls will be offered on your altar. (Psalm 51)

CONFESSION

He stood in front of me, cheeks flushed, his eyes glassy and wide. I knew he'd disobeyed, but he stood there, denying it to my face. I asked him twice, but he held to his lie.

I sent him away, "you need to think about what is happening right now," I told him. A few minutes later, I called him back. "Let's try this again," I suggested. "Tell me what you were doing, and be honest about it." He shrugged, his eyes fixed hard on the floor.

"You already know," he mumbled.

I did know, but I needed him to own it. This was one of those teachable parenting moments that we could not afford to ignore.

"I need you to say it to me, I need you to tell me the truth." I waited silently. His lips trembled as tears leapt from his eyes. With his face still bent towards the floor, the confession spilled out of him. It was as I expected, we both knew it, and still the confession was necessary. Pulling him to my chest I held him in his shame. I forgave him, and in that moment, peace between us was restored.

Jesus's last hours in the garden of Gethsemane serve as a powerful example to us regarding the necessity of honest prayers and communication with God. Though Jesus had no confession to make, He reveals His humanity as He prays fervently in preparation for enduring His crucifixion. His garden prayers are those of deep anguish—rather than an admission of wrongdoing, Christ empties his thoughts and feelings out to His Father.

"My Father, if it is possible, may this cup be taken from me.
Yet not as I will, but as you will" (Matthew 26:39).

Jesus tells His disciples that He is "overwhelmed with sorrow to the point of death." Here in the crushing place, He demonstrates what surrender looks like: "Yet not as I will, but as you will."

Though He is clearly troubled by the coming horror of His crucifixion, He demonstrates willing obedience. While most of us will likely never know the terror of facing a literal crucifixion, the death to self (Luke 9:23-24) that God calls each of us to can feel crushing. We have heard someone say that they'd "rather die" than have a certain truth uncovered about them. Maybe we've even said this ourselves. Confession puts us in a state of vulnerability, which for most of us can be so terrifyingly uncomfortable that we avoid it altogether or rationalize away our need to confess at all.

After all, God already knows all about our sin. (And no creature is hidden from his sight, but all are naked and exposed to the eyes of him to whom we must give account. Hebrews 4:13)

For some of us, shame tightens the noose around our neck, and we live afraid that our admission of guilt would be the sudden jerk to our death. Confession, however, leads to life. Open, repentant confession before God serves as the gateway to freedom. Confession allows for forgiveness, which makes us receptive to the redemptive work of Christ.

When His mercy infiltrates our hearts we turn from being focused on our sins, to being focused on the Son.

READ & REFLECT

READ LUKE 9:23-24

And he said to all, "If anyone would come after me, let him deny himself and take up his cross daily and follow me. For whoever would save his life will lose it, but whoever loses his life for my sake will save it.

1. We are eager for Easter. We can't wait for that sunrise. But, before this glorious celebration comes the preparation. Without the crucifixion, there would be no Easter Sunday. The celebration is a gift, which came with the ultimate price tag. Jesus has some difficult words for us regarding the price of fellowship with Him. What does it look like in your life to deny yourself?

2. What does it mean to you to carry your cross?

3. What does surrender look like in your life?

READ 1 JOHN 1:6-9

If we say we have fellowship with him while we walk in darkness, we lie and do not practice the truth. But if we walk in the light, as he is in the light, we have fellowship with one another, and the blood of Jesus his Son cleanses us from all sin. If we say we have no sin, we deceive ourselves, and the truth is not in us. If we confess our sins, he is faithful and just to forgive us our sins and to cleanse us from all unrighteousness.

4. As a lit lamp transforms a darkened room, so are we called to be a light in the darkness of this fallen world. As "light-bearers" (Matthew 5:14), we cannot truly live life apart from confession. What does this passage from 1 John say about us when we deny the need for confession and repentance?

5. What does this passage say about God? What are the two things we are told follow our confession of sin? What has this cleansing looked like in your life (write about a particular experience)?

READ PROVERBS 28:13

Whoever conceals his transgressions will not prosper, but he who confesses and forsakes them will obtain mercy.

6. How does knowing this about God make you feel about the necessity of confessing your sins and accepting the forgiveness God willingly offers for a repentant soul?

7. In the section Get on Your Face, I described a difficult awakening to the repeat sin of pride in my life. The feeling of conviction can be utterly painful when God reveals sins that we have overlooked or ignored. Recall a time when you experienced God's merciful conviction. What was that experience like for you? How did God use that to stretch and grow your faith?

READ 1 CORINTHIANS 1: 25-31

For the foolishness of God is wiser than men, and the weakness of God is stronger than men. For consider your calling, brothers: not many of you were wise according to worldly standards, not many were powerful, not many were of noble birth. But God chose what is foolish in the world to shame the wise; God chose what is weak in the world to shame the strong; God chose what is low and despised in the world, even things that are not, to bring to nothing things that are, so that no human being might boast in the presence of God. And because of him you are in Christ Jesus, who became to us wisdom from God, righteousness and sanctification and redemption, so that, as it is written, "Let the one who boasts, boast in the Lord."

8. Our pride sometimes threatens our ability to be vulnerable in our confession. Admitting failure can feel like weakness. In this passage, what does Paul say God does with weakness?

9. Consider the vast flawed men and women of the Old Testament whom God intentionally placed in roles of leadership, and to whom He burdened with tremendous responsibility (Moses, David, Saul, Rahab, etc). God deliberately raises up the weak for His purposes. Clearly the flaws we find difficult to stomach in ourselves, God uses for His purposes. Our sinful tendencies are not an obstacle for God. Does this truth come as a relief? Take some time and pray about one particular area where you struggle repeatedly. Ask God to use this weakness for His purposes.

10. Have you experienced God's redemption of a weakness in your own life? Take some time to think of a specific example.

11. How does realizing God's willingness to use us, in spite of ourselves, make you feel about the need to confess your weakness and struggles to Him? Are you more willing? Less? Does it make confession easier?

12. Looking back at 1 Corinthians 1:30, what does it say about who Jesus became to us? (Try reading this verse out loud, so that your ears can hear it. How does it feel to hear this blessed truth?)

READ HEBREWS 12:5-13

And have you forgotten the exhortation that addresses you as sons? "My son, do not regard lightly the discipline of the Lord, nor be weary when reproved by him. For the Lord disciplines the one he loves, and chastises every son whom he receives." It is for discipline that you have to endure. God is treating you as sons. For what son is there whom his father does not discipline? If you are left without discipline, in which all have participated, then you are illegitimate children and not sons. Besides this, we have had earthly fathers who disciplined us and we respected them. Shall we not much more be subject to the Father of spirits and live? For they disciplined us for a short time as it seemed best to them, but he disciplines us for our good, that we may share his holiness. For the moment all discipline seems painful rather than pleasant, but later it yields the peaceful fruit of righteousness to those who have been trained by it. Therefore lift your drooping hands and strengthen your weak knees, and make straight paths for your feet, so that what is lame may not be put out of joint but rather be healed.

13. Discipline is often unpleasant—ask my children, or any child for that matter. Most of us don't rejoice over being corrected, and yet we are told here that one of the ways God loves us is by disciplining us. Our struggles are often God's way of refining us for His purposes. When our will stands strong in the face of God's call on our lives, when we resist His loving discipline, we render ourselves impotent in the Kingdom. There is work to be done—specific kingdom work God is calling you to, right now, in this very moment. How do you receive His discipline? What is produced as a result of being trained by God's discipline?

14. What does Paul say comes from "making level paths for your feet"? What can we come to understand about the benefits of the refining process by reading this scripture?

As we wander through this Lenten season, we may (and hopefully will) find ourselves at the crushing place. This is a place not for fear, but for freedom. Confession of our doubts and struggles loosens the chains of sin and sends us further into the fires of refinement and deeper on our journey of sanctification. Here in this place, we weep with the anguish of a soul that has seen the depths of our own depravity. We weep with Christ, with honest sorrow and ridiculous joy so that, as we let it all out, we will walk out of the garden freer than when we stumbled in.

Prayer Prompts

Thank God for the gift of Jesus as our sacrificial lamb. Spend a few minutes giving thanks for the specific aspects of Jesus's life and death that you are most grateful for in these moments.

Ask for God to strengthen you to face the things He is currently working on in you. Ask Him to specifically remove obstacles that keep you from surrendering more fully to Him.

Pray for the strength to face the cross in your life, and to carry it by His strength, for His glory.

27

DEEP SORROW (REPENTANCE)

As they were walking along the road, a man said to him, "I will follow you wherever you go." Jesus replied, "Foxes have dens and birds have nests, but the Son of Man has no place to lay his head." He said to another man, "Follow me." But he replied, "Lord, first let me go and bury my father." Jesus said to him, "Let the dead bury their own dead, but you go and proclaim the kingdom of God." Still another said, "I will follow you, Lord; but first let me go back and say goodbye to my family." Jesus replied, "No one who puts a hand to the plow and looks back is fit for service in the kingdom of God."

(Luke 9:57-62)

Pray

Jesus we come with our dirty hands and our stained hearts, with nothing worthy to offer. Help us to turn from our sin, to lay aside the distractions of our affections, and walk whole-heartedly towards you. Change our minds, Lord. Turn our hearts towards you. Amen.

METANOEO

The Greek word for repentance is metanoeo, a word which when translated means, "to think differently after." This word for repentance is a turning from the old ways of thinking and living, to the new way—Christ's way. This is what we are called to. This changed way of thinking is the mark of true repentance.

Obedient Christian living is marked with repentance. It is not a one-time occurrence. We turn again and again, throughout our lives from the sin that infiltrates our hearts. This turning, this thinking differently afterwards, is the hardline of our faith. We cannot serve two masters, and so in serving Christ we turn from the other idols that vie for our affections. Jesus tells us not to look back. This passage in particular is a straightforward call to utter devotion to Jesus—alone. In pursuing gospel living, we are forced to prioritize our gaze. Christ becomes our home. Our devotion is for Him. He, our sole point of focus.

READ & REFLECT

READ EZEKIEL 33:10-20

"And you, son of man, say to the house of Israel, Thus have you said: 'Surely our transgressions and our sins are upon us, and we rot away because of them. How then can we live?' Say to them, As I live, declares the Lord God, I have no pleasure in the death of the wicked, but that the wicked turn from his way and live; turn back, turn back from your evil ways, for why will you die, O house of Israel?

"And you, son of man, say to your people, The righteousness of the righteous shall not deliver him when he transgresses, and as for the wickedness of the wicked, he shall not fall by it when he turns from his wickedness, and the righteous shall not be able to live by his righteousness when he sins. Though I say to the righteous that he shall surely live, yet if he trusts in his righteousness and does injustice, none of his righteous deeds shall be remembered, but in his injustice that he has done he shall die. Again, though I say to the wicked, 'You shall surely die,' yet if he turns from his sin and does what is just and right, if the wicked restores the pledge, gives back what he has taken by robbery, and walks in the statutes of life, not doing injustice, he shall surely live; he shall not die. None of the sins that he has committed shall be remembered against him. He has done what is just and right; he shall surely live.

"Yet your people say, 'The way of the Lord is not just,' when it is their own way that is not just. When the righteous turns from his righteousness and does injustice, he shall die for it. And when the wicked turns from his wickedness and does what is just and right, he shall live by this. Yet you say, 'The way of the Lord is not just.' O house of Israel, I will judge each of you according to his ways."

1. Sin leads to death. The Israelites experienced this countless times on their journey from Egypt to the Promise Land. (We read this again later in Romans 6:23.) Here, Ezekiel is being charged with the responsibility of warning

the people to turn from their sins, lest they be cast down forever. Our casual sins are not unnoticed by the Lord. The call to repentance is not one to be taken lightly, or smoothed over with the notions of grace, mercy, and unfailing love. This is the very benchmark of a Christian: a surrendered, repentant heart. In this passage, God gives Ezekiel a passionate message, a plea for salvation and an image of what God's justice looks like. What kinds of thoughts do you have as you read this passage? How does this impact your views of God's righteous judgment and His idea of justice?

2. This passage reveals a bit of what God's justice looks like. What does He say the wicked must do? What is the result for them if they do this?

READ 2 PETER 3:9

The Lord is not slow to fulfill his promise as some count slowness, but is patient toward you, not wishing that any should perish, but that all should reach repentance.

3. While God instructs Ezekiel to give an impassioned call for repentance, here Peter reminds us that God is patient with us. God cares deeply for our souls and as such calls us directly to Himself by way of repentance. He is patient with us, knowing that we are frail and weak. He knows that even as our hearts long to live under the banner of His love, repentance for some comes slow. God is not wanting anyone to perish, but everyone to come to repentance (2 Peter 3:9b). God is patient. What are you

holding back from the Lord? What do you need to turn from right now that distracts you in pursuit of Christ?

READ MATTHEW 3:1-8

In those days John the Baptist came preaching in the wilderness of Judea, "Repent, for the kingdom of heaven is at hand." For this is he who was spoken of by the prophet Isaiah when he said,

"The voice of one crying in the wilderness:
'Prepare the way of the Lord;
make his paths straight.'"

Now John wore a garment of camel's hair and a leather belt around his waist, and his food was locusts and wild honey. Then Jerusalem and all Judea and all the region about the Jordan were going out to him, and they were baptized by him in the river Jordan, confessing their sins. But when he saw many of the Pharisees and Sadducees coming to his baptism, he said to them, "You brood of vipers! Who warned you to flee from the wrath to come? Bear fruit in keeping with repentance."

4. There were 400 quiet years between the words found in Malachi at the end of the Old Testament, and the words of John the Baptist in the New Testament. The book of Matthew opens with the call to repentance. Apart from the brief genealogical history of Christ and the story of His birth, repentance is the first message God has for us after 400 years of apparent silence. John calls out, "repent," in preparation for Christ's coming. We are called to this same repentance in expectation of Christ's imminent return. He

is coming back, just as He said. Do you feel ready for Christ's return? What preparations could you take today to make your heart ready for His coming?

5. Matthew says in vs. 8, "bear fruit in keeping with repentance." What do you think this means? How does this statement relate to the concept of metanoeo? What does the fruit of repentance look like in your life?

READ ISAIAH 58

"Cry aloud; do not hold back; lift up your voice like a trumpet; declare to my people their transgression, to the house of Jacob their sins. Yet they seek me daily and delight to know my ways, as if they were a nation that did righteousness and did not forsake the judgment of their God; they ask of me righteous judgments; they delight to draw near to God. 'Why have we fasted, and you see it not? Why have we humbled ourselves, and you take no knowledge of it?' Behold, in the day of your fast you seek your own pleasure, and oppress all your workers. Behold, you fast only to quarrel and to fight and to hit with a wicked fist. Fasting like yours this day will not make your voice to be heard on high. Is such the fast that I choose, a day for a person to humble himself? Is it to bow down his head like a reed, and to spread sackcloth and ashes under him? Will you call this a fast, and a day acceptable to the Lord? "Is not this the fast that I choose: to loose the bonds of wickedness, to undo the straps of the yoke, to let the oppressed go free, and to break every yoke? Is it not to share your bread with the hungry and bring the homeless poor into your house; when you see the naked, to cover him, and not to hide yourself from your own flesh? Then shall your light break forth like the dawn, and your healing shall spring up speedily; your righteousness shall go before you; the glory of the Lord shall be your rear guard. Then you shall call, and the Lord will answer; you shall cry, and he will say, 'Here I am.' If you take away the yoke from your midst, the pointing of the finger, and speaking wickedness, if you pour yourself out for the hungry and satisfy the desire of the afflicted, then shall your light rise in the darkness and your gloom be as the noonday. And the Lord will guide you continually and satisfy your desire in scorched places and make your bones strong; and you shall be like a watered garden, like a spring of water, whose waters do not fail. And your ancient ruins shall be rebuilt; you shall raise up the foundations of many generations; you shall be called the repairer of the breach, the restorer of streets to dwell in. "If you turn back your foot from the Sabbath, from doing your pleasure on my holy day, and call the Sabbath a delight and the holy day of the Lord honorable; if you honor it, not going your own ways, or seeking your own pleasure, or talking idly; then you shall take delight in the Lord, and I will make you ride on the heights of the earth; I will feed you with the heritage of Jacob your father, for the mouth of the Lord has spoken."

6. In this passage, God calls the Israelites out for the way they have been fasting. How does God describe the kind of fasting that honors Him?

7. What is the response God tells the Israelites to expect when they fast in this way? What does this kind of fasting

experience sound like to you? Do you think it would be a joyful experience?

READ MATTHEW 6:16-18

"And when you fast, do not look gloomy like the hypocrites, for they disfigure their faces that their fasting may be seen by others. Truly, I say to you, they have received their reward. But when you fast, anoint your head and wash your face, that your fasting may not be seen by others but by your Father who is in secret. And your Father who sees in secret will reward you.

8. Compare the fasting God talks about in Isaiah 58 with the kind of fasting the "hypocrites" Jesus is talking about here are engaged in. What is the attitude God wants us to reflect when we fast?

9. Think about the last time you fasted. What was your reason for the fast? What was the experience like for you? How did this fast impact your relationship with God?

10. If you have never fasted, why not? How do you feel about fasting as a spiritual practice after reading these scriptures?

Why not come to Him? Allow yourself to come empty, refraining from that which only gives temporary satisfaction and let Him fill you.

Prayer Prompts

Thank God for His patient mercy. Take time to reflect on the joy and gratitude you feel when you recount His gracious forgiveness of your sins.

Ask God to bring to mind any remaining unrepentant sin in your life. As things come to mind, confess them to Him (and to others if necessary) and receive His forgiveness.

Pray for the strength to resist the temptations of this world. Ask God to equip you and prepare you for the daily struggles that come with living in a broken place. Believe that He will not abandon you in your time of need, and that by Christ's death and resurrection, you are indeed under the cover of grace. Consider fasting for a brief time. Ask God to guide you and speak to you as you seek Him through fasting.

28

NEW LIFE (ATONEMENT)

He prunes us so we will bear fruit. For Him. For His kingdom, not ours. Our faith is purified so God will be glorified.

(Holey, Wholly, Holy)

Pray

Heavenly Father, You have put eternity in our hearts and created us with specific intention. We cannot know the depths of Your wonder, nor the full majesty of Your glory, but yet You call us to embrace You with both arms, with our whole hearts. Though on our own we fail, the shed blood of Christ covers us fully. For this we can only fall at Your feet in awe and praise. Amen.

By His Strength, For His Glory

"You are not the main character of your life story." That's what I told the kids sitting in the basement youth room during a weekend retreat I'd been invited to speak at. It hit me there, looking out at this small gathering of teenagers, how often I've lived as the star of my life. I sometimes believe it all revolves around me. But it doesn't. Because when it does, it all falls apart. I am no sun and my center of gravity shifts with my ever-changing moods. I tilt and spin and fall. I tip and flail and stumble and break wide open under pressure.

"Jesus is the center of your story—God, the author." Our life's purpose is to give God glory—that's the whole thing, condensed into eight words. This is the sum total of our reason for being.

Our unworthiness may feel overwhelming, particularly as we have descended into the depths of our faults and failures. We've seen the ugliness of our hearts and laid it bare before the cross. We've stood naked and ashamed, without excuse or defense. The curtain is torn—the veil removed. In his final act of love, Christ's blood flows from the cross down over us, bent at His feet. A ribbon of red warmth curls and wraps around us. The ribbon expands and its warmth emanates from our shoulders to our toes, without realizing it, we find ourselves no longer naked but clothed—covered in a robe of righteousness. His shed blood, our new covering. He is in us, and we, in Him. Who is it God sees when He looks at us? Why, it's Christ.

He doesn't see our sin, He sees His Son.

READ & REFLECT

READ 2 CORINTHIANS 3:12-18

Since we have such a hope, we are very bold, not like Moses, who would put a veil over his face so that the Israelites might not gaze at the outcome of what was being brought to an end. But their minds were hardened. For to this day, when they read the old covenant, that same veil remains un-lifted, because only through Christ is it taken away. Yes, to this day whenever Moses is read a veil lies over their hearts. But when one turns to the Lord, the veil is removed. Now the Lord is the Spirit, and where the Spirit of the Lord is, there is freedom. And we all, with unveiled face, beholding the glory of the Lord, are being transformed into the same image from one degree of glory to another. For this comes from the Lord who is the Spirit (2 Corinthians 3:12-18).

1. Before Christ, a veil existed to shield the Israelites from God's glory. In the temples, a veil separated the people from the holy of holies. How does Paul say the veil is removed? What is happening to us as we move through our days, inching ever closer to union with Christ?

READ 1 TIMOTHY 2:5

For there is one God, and there is one mediator between God and men, the man Christ Jesus...

2. Upon the completion of the crucifixion, Matthew 27:50-51 states: And when Jesus had cried out again in a loud

voice, he gave up his spirit. At that moment the curtain of the temple was torn in two from top to bottom. Looking at 1 Timothy 2:5, what does Timothy say about our access to the Father? How does knowing that the veil is gone impact your view of holiness?

READ ISAIAH 61:10

I will greatly rejoice in the Lord; my soul shall exult in my God, for he has clothed me with the garments of salvation; he has covered me with the robe of righteousness, as a bridegroom decks himself like a priest with a beautiful headdress, and as a bride adorns herself with her jewels.

3. Close your eyes. Thinking about the passage you just read, what do you see? How does this image fit with the thoughts you have about yourself when you pass a mirror? How does this reality of being clothed in garments of salvation and righteousness feel to you?

READ JOHN 15:2-8

Every branch in me that does not bear fruit he takes away, and every branch that does bear fruit he prunes, that it may bear more fruit. Already you are clean because of the word that I have spoken to you. Abide in me, and I in you. As the branch cannot bear fruit by itself, unless it abides in the vine, neither can you, unless you abide in me. I am the vine; you are the branches. Whoever abides in me and I in him, he it is that bears much fruit, for apart from me you can do nothing. If anyone does not abide in me he is thrown away like a branch and withers; and the branches are gathered, thrown into the fire, and burned. If you abide in me, and my words abide in you, ask whatever you wish, and it will be done for you. By this my Father is glorified, that you bear much fruit and so prove to be my disciples.

4. For what purpose do we endure the hard pruning of our lives? What has this purposeful pruning looked like in your life? How have you seen the fruit of God's labor in your heart? How does knowing the purpose behind the process affect your perspective on enduring the hard pruning that is sometimes necessary to grow you in your faith?

READ 1 PETER 1:3-7

Blessed be the God and Father of our Lord Jesus Christ! According to his great mercy, he has caused us to be born again to a living hope through the resurrection of Jesus Christ from the dead, to an inheritance that is imperishable, undefiled, and unfading, kept in heaven for you, who by God's power are being guarded through faith for a salvation ready to be revealed in the last time. In this you rejoice, though now for a little while, if necessary, you have been grieved by various trials, so that the tested genuineness of your faith—more precious than gold that perishes though it is tested by fire—may be found to result in praise and glory and honor at the revelation of Jesus Christ.

5. Peter's words sound joyful as He encourages us to remain faithful during the hard refining of our hearts. How do you feel when you read this passage? Does it make you

want to rejoice, even as you may be suffering? Does it give you hope to hear of God's intent for you?

Prayer Points

Spend a few minutes thanking God for His merciful work of pruning your heart. Ask Him to help you endure the challenge of letting go and to help you celebrate His redemptive work in your life.

Consider the ways you struggle to let God work out His salvation in your life and heart. Pray about those parts of your life that you may be holding onto too tightly.

Invite God to tale the burdens you're carrying in this season, from you. Ask for His help to surrender and for Him to teach you what it means to abide in Him.

29

EASTER PEOPLE

"Do not abandon yourselves to despair. We are the Easter people and hallelujah is our song."
Pope John Paul II

Easter, at long last. We've picked our way through the desert and brambles of self-reflection. We've eyed the gaping holes in our hearts and wept over the broken places and spaces that have long needed filling. We've waited imperfectly in the garden of Gethsemane and landed face-first at the foot of a cross that weighed more than we could bear. Our hearts have been broken and mended, emptied and filled, cut wide open and stitched right up with threads of purest grace. We've hunched outside the tomb and waited for resurrection—one we didn't even know was coming. We've doubted and feared, we've needed proof—and so we've touched the very holes that held Him to it. The holes responsible for our holiness. We wear a ribbon of finest crimson. A robe knit from His flesh and dyed with His blood. We're whiter than we've ever been; the fullers' soap has rubbed the filth away.

We are the Easter people. The people made for glory—we rejoice in His victory, Hallelujah is our song.

A NOTE FOR SMALL
GROUP LEADERS

Because our refinement journey's are often intensely personal, it is important to create and facilitate an environment of trust. Adopting a philosophy of privacy for whatever is shared during meetings and discussion sessions is paramount for those who are on this journey with you.

Avoid judgmental statements—instead of focusing on the sins and struggles of your fellows in the faith, remember to emphasize the transformative power available to all through the shed blood of Jesus Christ. Wherever we are in our own personal journey, the hope of redemption exists as long as we have breath in our lungs.

Therefore encourage one another and build each other up, just as in fact you are doing (1 Thessalonians 5:11).

BIBLIOGRAPHY

1. Bonhoeffer, Dietrich. The Cost of Discipleship. London: SCM Press, 1948/2001.
2. Capon, Robert. The supper of the lamb : a culinary reflection. New York: Modern Library, 2002.
3. Manning, Brennan, John Blase, and Philip Yancey. *All Is Grace: A Ragamuffin Memoir*. Colorado Springs, CO: David C. Cook, 2011.
4. Tozer, A.W. The pursuit of God. S.l: W.L.C, 2009.
5. Wangerin, Walter. Reliving the passion : meditations on the suffering, death, and resurrection of Jesus as recorded in Mark. Grand Rapids, Mich: Zondervan Pub. House, 1992.

Companion Workbook Sources

http://www.computerworld.com/s/article/9216644/ Many_Android_iPhone_users_run_mobile_apps_before_getting_out_of_bed

[1] http://www.dailymail.co.uk/news/article-2117987/Lost-today-Misplaced-items-cost-minutes-day.html

[1]http://www.americanbible.org/uploads/content/ State%20of%20the%20Bible%20Report%202013.pdf

[1] Harry Ironside, "Except Ye Repent", http://www.jesus-is-savior.com/BTP/Dr_Harry_Ironside/Except_Ye_Repent/01.htm

HOLEY, WHOLLY, HOLY

ABOUT THE AUTHOR

As a sequin-wearing, homeschooling mother of four, Kris is passionate about Jesus, people and words. Her heart beats to share the hard, but glorious truth about life in Christ. She's been known to take gratuitous pictures of her culinary creations, causing mouths to water all across Instagram. Once upon a time, she ran 10 miles for Compassion International, a ministry for which she serves as an advocate. She is the author of Come, Lord Jesus: The Weight of Waiting, and has contributed to multiple other published works. Her writing has been featured on numerous blogs around the web. She spends her free time managing GraceTable.org and writing at kriscamealy.com.

Connect with Kris:
Facebook: http://facebook.com/krisecamealy
Twitter: http://twitter.com/kriscamealy
Instagram: @kriscamealy

OTHER BOOKS

Finding Church: Stories of Finding, Switching, and Reforming (Civitas Press, 2012)

Holey, Wholly, Holy: A Lenten Journey Of refinement (Create Space 2013)

Holey Holey, Wholly: A Lenten Journey of Refinement, Companion Workbook (Create Space 2014)

Soul Bare: Stories of redemption (Contributor, IVP, 2016)

Craving Connection: 30 Challenges For real Life Engagement (Contributor, B&H Books, 2017)

The Heart of Marriage: Stories That Celebrate The Adventure Of Life Together (Contributor, Revell, 2017)

ALSO AVAILABLE

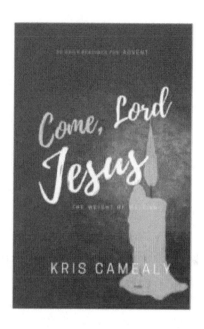

Made in the USA
Las Vegas, NV
20 January 2022

41900309R00085